How To Fall

KAREN ANNESEN grew up on Cape Cod, Massachusetts. Selections of her work have appeared in *The Like of It* (Baring & Rogerson, 2005) and *Oxford Poets 2004: An Anthology* (Carcanet). She has degrees in Psychology, Housing and Writing, and has taught Creative Writing and worked with homeless women and people with learning disabilities in London and Oxfordshire, where she now lives.

How To Fall

KAREN ANNESEN

*for Nicole
with all best wishes
for you & your poetry*

Karen Annesen

SALT

CAMBRIDGE

PUBLISHED BY SALT PUBLISHING
14a High Street, Fulbourn, Cambridge CB21 5DH United Kingdom

The right of Karen Annesen to be identified as the
author of this work has been asserted by her in accordance
with Section 77 of the Copyright, Designs and Patents Act 1988.

Salt Publishing 2009

Printed in Great Britain by the MPG Books Group,
Bodmin and King's Lynn

Typeset in Swift 9.5 / 13

ISBN 978 1 84471 433 9 paperback

Salt Publishing Ltd gratefully acknowledges
the financial assistance of Arts Council England

1 3 5 7 9 8 6 4 2

for Mia

Contents

"Each one of us, then, should speak of his roads, his roadside benches; each one of us should make a surveyor's map of his lost fields and meadows."
— GASTON BACHELARD, *The Poetics of Space*

Acknowledgements

Acknowledgements are due to the editors of the following publications in which some of these poems first appeared: *Exeter Prize Anthology* (Odyssey Press), *Feminist Review*, *Limelight*, *Oxford Magazine*, *Oxford Poets 2004: An Anthology* (Carcanet), *Piano On Fire*, *PN Review*, *Poetry Scotland*, *The Like of It* (Baring and Rogerson, 2005), *The Magazine*, *The Picayune*, *The Yellow Crane*. 'Fishmonger's Café' was shortlisted for the Barnet Prize 2002, and 'Fair Promises' won second prize in the 2004 Yorkshire Open Poetry Competition.

Thanks to Carole Bromley, Helen Farish, Scott Harney, Denise Inge, Liane Strauss, Andy Ward, Mark Wood and Tamar Yoseloff as well as to my family. I am very grateful to everyone at the University of Glamorgan MPhil in Writing programme, especially Sheenagh Pugh.

I am also grateful to the Hawthornden Foundation for awarding me a Hawthornden Fellowship and to the Centre for Writers and Translators in Rhodes.

How to Fall

Easy, I've been doing it all my life.
On cobblestone streets
in high heels, yes.
Off a bike at seven,
your friend shouting *faster*
some fear mixing in your blood
with yellow cake and pink icing.
      Try a slapstick fall—
the ones where bodies
seem without bones,
seem to give way
somewhere low down.
Practice falling while smiling—
not wondering about your teeth,
the position of the furniture,
brain damage.
      Off a train, out of a speeding car
like a stunt artist.
Remember to look like someone else,
like someone who doesn't fall for a living.
Then, when those moving trains no longer scare you,
try falling out of love
with the one person
in whose eyes the world seems steady.

10.45 to Stockholm

In the dining car a woman sits alone in a booth,
her white hair wisping into a lunch
she eats from a margarine box.
No crusts and, when she leaves, no crumbs.

A few cars on, a sleeping woman in peach
paddles back down rivers,
tries to reach her green past
but always, just before, there are rapids.

A man distracts himself
recalling the waitress at breakfast.
Blonde hair teased its way
down the whole of her lithe back.

A child stands backwards on the seat
squealing in Swedish
to a Japanese couple behind. His hands move toys
up and down on some great journey.

Outside birch and quaking aspens,
wooden houses and shimmering lakes.
This could be home, New Hampshire or Maine.
Dirt tracks lead nowhere in any language.

Wishing

The boat lay low, weighted
by young bodies which rocked
the dark lake each time they moved.

Above, they hoped, were stars
waiting to die and in that dying
yield up a wish for her, for him

for anyone out that August night.
The moon was half-full, half-empty.
Crickets played a persistent tune.

They were almost asleep and then—
a bright arc across the sky.
A dog barked, crickets paused.

They rowed back wide awake,
believing in wishes,
parting black water.

Fishmonger's Café

Mussels jostle in bowls.
Lobster, corn on the cob,
everything, especially the man
you are with, drips butter.

Outside a bridge rises
and lowers for boats.
Either warm air or chilled wine
sends your mind back
to summers watching
this bridge, the boats,
the waitresses kissing the cooks—
mint mocha ice cream slipping
down your chin.

Tonight, at the Fishmonger's café
with your yellow dress and the moon,
take your turn.
Slip to that water's edge,
kiss his buttery lips.

Bridesmaid

Her veil blows across my face,
my hand tight in hers on the way to church.
We might be skipping along, seven and eight
except for that veil. The lace scratches
and I wonder again about her choice.
Why white at twenty-nine?

Mr Miller's cutting the lawn while his wife weeds
the borders humming a tune I can't make out.
I'm in apricot, last time pink.
My hand is sweating, or is it hers?
The church will be cool,
Father Peter's eyes will look past mine.

It's time. We enter and I smooth her dress,
ease the veil over her soft flushed face.

The Dunes

If you stay in that house you'll fossilize.
Get the purple bike, pedal fast
to the honeysuckle path.
Then rest a moment — tease
the golden centres out and taste —
no wine will ever match that clear liquid.

Look into the window at Patrick's. He's not there.
Carry on alone (best get used to it)
and stop again by the grey pier
where water laps the rowing boats.

The smell of ice cream and sunscreen
is thick now and seagulls call overhead.
The pavement is half-covered in sand.
Pass the street where Loni will steal flowers
and blame you, pass the boys diving off the bridge
(soon they'll shout words you won't understand).

Ease your body into the shallow water.
The sun is on your back.
Beach grass bends in a breeze.
Below you your handprints appear and disappear,
appear and disappear in wet sand.

Playground

Teacher's pet, Teacher's pet
my friend was saying, her voice
as flat as our chests at twelve.
After the first slap
I knew this was a real fight,
the whole class was clapping
and no teachers would hear in time.

This was East coast suburbia, spring 1976,
Jimmy Carter trying
to talk sense in an accent no one took seriously.
Batons would twirl
in Bicentennial parades in every small town.
Olympics. Nadia Comaneci would bend us
into a rare American silence.

On the playground the shouting grew louder, my hands
pulled hair, clawed skin and found soft places to hit.
After years of fending off an older brother
I knew I'd never win, but I wouldn't quit either.
Maybe the bell rang, maybe they got bored.
You're not a bad fighter, you know, my friend
said, smiling. And then it was over.

Carl's Bar and Grill

She sits another night at Carl's bar.
Only drunks come out on nights like this.
She'd never known nights so long or so cold
or a bar so warm. The silence came in waves.
The butcher's wife is pregnant
again, but he was 'done' after the fourth.
The price of logs gone up.

By spring she'd leave she knew—and they guessed.
Carl asked one night, which was better, arriving or leaving?
Oh, leaving for sure.
Arriving is always the same sweet mix of promises.
Leaving, well, you never know a person or a place
until you leave.

Getting On

He's young and insatiable,
but we are not alone in the room.
Others walk in and out:
my mother who says *You're getting on*
you know, a leggy Italian called Maria,
members of his band looking
for somewhere to practice.
Men who want to marry me
bring colour charts and names for children.
They have DIY plans and business cards.
I pull the duvet over our heads,
tell the band to play on.

Via London

One shoe slips into dull brown mud.
New asphalt steams from machines
held steady by three men in orange—
the racket drowns out our seagulls.
A black cab going the other way
spins around, takes us to Waverly Station.

I wait as you negotiate
a change of plan via London.
You are at that window so long
that I notice whole lives:
the strange older couple in trench coats,
hats pulled down. Dark leather gloves
clutch the handles of two immaculate fawn cases.
A thin boy with glasses whines at his mother.
In ten years time he will stand here silent
hug her and not glance back.

The red numbers of the digital clock move
with undue speed. The board tells me
London Kings Cross is Platform 19.
You are still at that window.
I blink hard to forget the blue-eyed baby
gliding by in her pram.

We will be in London at 2.57.
Another black cab, another few hours together.
Later, I will take
a smooth cloth, remove
all traces of mud from my shoe.

Late Night Window

This dark comes hours
after day. Layer upon layer
of light withdrawn.

A house stands alone on a hill
sending its inner light out.
Some meagre measure

of thick black dissipates.
We see edges of the house,
the line of the eaves.

What we cannot see, we hear.
Owls, bats. The grass we know
from experience is wet.

Our small lives make us watch
for figures at the window.
A man and a woman argue.

We walk the mile back
and sleep reassured we are not alone.
A streetlamp pierces the thin curtains.

A Boy Can Dream of Honey Only If He's Tasted It

The boy idles along a narrow path
pulling at beach plums.
At the end the path widens for a view of the sea
he'll never tire of remembering.
One day he'll whisper all the names of grasses
into a girl's ear in a meadow: Foxtail, Maiden, Upland Sea.

The city will have its pleasures too,
but on a summer's night
it will not be a fan's dead hum
sending him to sleep, but the sound of the sea
lapping at rocks,
filling all the spaces it has carved for itself.

Inside This Room

You whisper tales
of a younger you travelling
across my country. *Carolina*

you say, but now I am ready.
Boston, which you liked.
New York, which you didn't.

None gets me like that first *Nevada*.
I feel the hot sun,
the glint of it on chrome.

Outside it is cold even for Edinburgh.
A blue ship enters Leith harbour.
Men gather to guide it to a narrow berth.

Cheyenne, Little Rock, Cape Cod—
I could take you back there.
You hear what I am thinking, say

We're here now.
There are continents to explore
inside this room, *Nevada*.

Every Dark Place

Cast iron pans hung from hooks
over a Formica counter and below that a place of miracles
where a gluey mass became a risen loaf.
Nearby the wood-burning stove was fed and stirred.
The logs must be laid like this, Father would say
and Mother would nod agreement and do it her way.
The light pine shelves lined with tins of peas,
boxes of macaroni and bags of Pillsbury flour.

One day my sister stood on tiptoe, reached for a glass
and felt instead her hand on chocolate bars.
She searched for further secrets in every dark place
finding a rat who died for the love of cheese
and rows of old jam jars stuffed full of mother's stories,
half-finished, wet with time.

A Few Words

The old woman in black
watched me light the candle,
anchor it in the metal tray of sand,
drop some coins in the box
and stand before the flame.

When I turned she glanced away,
but, as I passed, she said a few words in Greek.
Perhaps *Thank you for the donation*
or *Take care*. I wanted her to say:
She is all right now, you will sleep again.

Cornmarket Street, Oxford

A gypsy grips you with her drooping eye.
She's pinned you to the wall, pressed
lavender under your nose.

For luck, she says as you rummage for coins.
Are you married? No.
Have you a good mother? Yes.

Take one for her too.
You've found two pounds, but she sees the mobile.
Give me three. Love will touch you again,

and there may be children. Her good eye knows she's
got you now.
Let me read your palm. But you're late. *I'm late.*

Let me put a crystal in your hand.
You're wavering.

The meeting is starting.

Fair Promises

Whatever I asked, she answered in proverbs.
She swept hard at the steps and didn't look up
when the men drove hounds
through town to the hunt. She said,
Not in war nor in peace
will a dead bee gather honey.

After he hit me, again, she said
Fair promises will make a fool happy
then baked enough Welsh cakes
for a month of cold nights.
One day the doctor came
too late. I told him,
Tomorrow is a stranger.

Unsteady

She left her bible behind
the night it rained and rained
and rained. They were somewhere
between Georgia and Alabama
when the car started to stutter

and shake then finally die.
He was getting grease on his jacket,
well it was his brother's really
and she who had felt like an angel
in her second-hand wedding gown

suddenly saw in the rear-view mirror
all that was and would be
and she wanted to speak then
and not hold her peace—
but the engine was roaring
and he was signing to her,
thumbs up, all is well.

At the Inn-Between

In the kitchen Dolce crisps chicken for twenty
in cast iron pans. My first taste of plantains
fried was here, it seems just nights ago,
even now I can feel them hot
and soft at the back of my throat.
In the hallway Joanne beats back at shadows,
bleaches black and white tiles nearly grey.
Downstairs Gladys teaches young mothers childcare
while one then two of her children die inside her.
I make the hostel a home
painting walls cranberry and cornflower.
No amount of colour alters Jane's pale stare.
With high heeled shoes
he drove tiny holes in every inch of her body
until she leaked her way here.

Dwyfor

If you walk through three gates
stick to the path along the river
there is a place
where white water
rushes past black rocks
nosing the air like seals.
The way is marked
with yellow leaves inlaid in wet earth.

If you let it, the sound
will drown
those noises in your head:
last night's shouts and silences
the sizzle of fish
burning in a cast iron pan.

Letter from Lasswade

Today I saw hailstones gather
on my window ledge.
My ledge for this one month
as I retreat in. If no words come,
will they throw me out? Will you?
Is it lips not words you need?
Perhaps. Our lips, old friends,
have not seen each other lately,
although between the lines of careful letters
an occasional message slips.

Now you have a wife, a condo,
a legal way to earn a living—
no more stealing lines from open skies.
A time to count on everything.
So is this it, nothing else for me to give to you,
you to me? Steeped as I am in all these books,
the answers refuse to stack up.

Not like the dinners you made
while I studied for exams at school,
elbows resting on the table painted black
to cover shadows of the woman living there before.
This problem is more a pot full of possibilities
and I am dipping in for answers
finding that, on a cold day,
nothing beats a good familiar stew.

Altered

There was an island. And the sea of course, that too.
How it crashed and sprayed and varied the tune.
The one that had always played in her head. Gone.

So when she met you, who was she to argue
with a sunset the colour of peach stones
and that easy sliver of a moon?

Afternoon, Rhodes

1 PM

A brown, bald man walks the shore
enters the sea and merges—
a strip of seaweed—
but when he tries to leave he falters,
the current pulling him back,
his arms raised to regain a balance
he never knew he'd miss.

2 PM

At Anthony's there are no women
and when you enter
there will be loud banter.
You will think of running. If you stay
the men will bring from under the counter
a bowl of flowers—daisies, a few red roses,
something yellow you can't place.

3 PM

On the side of the church
which should be open
a brown and a white pigeon
escape the heat and the cat
who sleeps lightly under the Jasmine.
One pecks or maybe kisses the other
who looks away towards the sea.

Telling the Story

They met skipping
stones across a swollen lake.

A small breeze teased the afternoon.
She watched his wrist twist and his body

bend into the throw, her pulse
moving in rhythm with the stones.

Years later when telling the story
she skipped over that part,

hastened to the way his bright eyes flashed
as he picked up the biggest rock

then lobbed it into the water
laughing at the way it made her jump.

Letter to Nate

Rain is the same no matter which continent
and lakes reflect old sounds:
You're not welcome. So we move on. Or stay.

In Lothian wind drives rain horizontal
into peach red stone. Rooks bring me presents:
some flowers or a feather.

On Lake Balaton a brass band plays
each night out of tune. In Windermere
girls in bright red dance by the bank of a stream.

Nate, I am back at that fork in the road,
the one you kept trying to find.

Domestic Fire

Smoke comes into the dream,
the one he has each night
where hunger makes him eat himself.
Father laughing.

He wakes wondering about the smoke,
then smells it in his room.
He grabs the photo of his mother
in the pewter frame, then runs.

Outside, the sound of fire engines braking
and neighbours screaming.
Three houses on fire.
Officers shouting to him: *Who's in the house?*

It's empty, he hears himself say,
The house has been empty for years.

Stirring

Beneath a sky unsure
whether to return to winter

or press on into spring,
they sit alone among the cherry blossom.

She picks at a petal,
lets its clarity of pink and white

steady her for looking into eyes
still as seas she used to watch for storms.

A wooden table lies
between them and if his hands

would only halfway cross it,
her clothes might find their way to grass.

In her fingers, the petal
bruises now to mauve.

As If She Thought

The day she flew out of the window
she was no longer worrying
about how hard it had become to breathe.
She thought instead about the rare
and infinite blue of the sky and the way
even complicated landscapes
seemed simple from above.
A crowd began to gather.
Police scurried here and there.
A fireman was lifted in a crane,
but spoke so softly she barely heard.
As she fell, people screamed.
She looked surprised, one woman said,
as if she thought she could fly.

Imagining Falmouth

I picture it small
like a toy town now,
sometimes a light icing
of sugar snow
or the houses baked hard
in sudden heat
and no one at home.

Seth is the only one left.
He roams the neighbourhood—
eyes even wilder now.
The sky a light blue.
The field Desi and I ended
a friendship in is open
and grass blows long in the breeze.

She Eats Cherries Slowly

allows her tongue to pierce
the red flesh, rolls
the cherry stone across her teeth

She eats cherries slowly

turns the stem round
and round in her fingers as
the juice pools and slides

She eats cherries slowly

examines the stone
before placing it
in the pile beside her

She eats cherries slowly
while thinking of him

Dinas Terrace

When you're lost in Aberystwyth on Christmas Eve
and the light is sliding, you might ask directions of anyone
even the man coming out of his home with a saucepan.
He doesn't know, says *Dinas means fortress in Welsh*.

His one front tooth juts toward you and a feather of white hair
floats on a wind that tastes of snow. Nearly at the edge,
as far west as you can go, how lost can you be?
A woman drives by in a rusted truck smiling widely to herself.

In bed, later, thinking of the man, the woman, the saucepan
you dream she proclaims her truck to be a fortress—
but you are humming some tune only just remembered.
Words tilt on the tip of your tongue.

Eating a Mango with My Mother

Is it ripe?
Yes, press here,
red or green the colour
doesn't matter, just feel.
We tear at the skin
juice running through our fingers.

One sweet wet bite
and we lose ourselves
forget the broken mirrors
midnight screams and this distance
between us.

For a moment
we are back in that first kitchen
licking batter
laughing and laughing
until we leap from our chairs
to find the cake browning
but not burnt.

We are just in time.

Core

Quickly now, find
the river by the trees,
drop the pills,
small as seed,
to fish who can't remember
long enough for fear.
Reach in to cold clear water
let it take you to the place
you planted mango, kumquat, lemon.
The trees are laden with a harvest
won from years on jagged stone.
Fruit for a hundred sleepless nights;
seed for a thousand years
in fertile ground.

Catherine Wheel

It is New Year's Eve
when you walk onto the balcony, see
the Alps rise like holograms
over concrete towers. Stars
startle a darkening sky.
At midnight someone lights a Catherine Wheel
and you run for safety.
It spins on an upright board—
the sparks turn red then green now gold diffracting.
Bonne année everyone says, kissing.
Is it only three years since you went into the garden,
saw your lover tilt her blonde head back,
kneel above your friend?
The moon over them bright, waning.

River Mouth

Meet me where the Leithen
joins the Tweed.
Bring enough to sustain us
this long hot afternoon:
a blanket from the Mill shop, oatcakes,
apples (show me again how to eat them whole),
butter, ham, and the stories you have yet to tell.

Leave the camera at home—
there are days that won't be captured
that way. And if we cannot hold
it in our minds then we don't deserve
such soft air,
this unexpected heat of May,
a stretch of river to ourselves.

Let's sit under the elm trees
where I'll take your burdens from you,
the blanket, food and paper
and those thoughts not left behind,
the ones about tomorrow and next year.
Meet me at Innerleithen.
Touch this river mouth with a kiss.

More Invisible Still

The world is full of mostly invisible things—
the boredom of the bus driver lurching
from stop to stop
or some woman from accounts phoning.
The joy felt every cold blue morning
is left unsaid.
And what makes us stay in grey places
when there are others that are blue,
that too is mostly invisible
except at times it becomes clear—
your lover's eye fills up with it,
you see at once it makes you visible.

Into the Woods

If a Romanian man kisses your hand, says
Your thigh curves like a river,
you can, if you wish,
step out of your life into a wood,
lie down among the bluebells
beside a rust coloured stream
made ripe with trout.
The taste of his blood will give you strength.
You could be anyone, say
I am only shadow, water follows me.
But if he asks: *What do you wish for?*
Will you say: *My life, just as it is?*

Waverly Station

The train does not want to leave,
protests with a slow chugging.

Can this be over?
It almost didn't begin.

The honeysuckle wasn't in bloom
as we'd expected. Who could have known

there would be such a determined grey?
The air tastes of singed hair: that split

second that cannot be relived.
You shout out the window: "Write,"

and we smile, our hands already
in our pockets fingering for words:

Sometimes even the fastest train
doesn't take you where you need to go,

or switched tracks, sorry
for any turbulence, or goodbye.

Coniston Water

The lake looks back, but says nothing.
Its cold grey eye blinks only in wind.

Today the air is still, a few walkers skim
the shore, saying, *It was luck the divers found her.*

Twenty years she lay weighted by bricks and a memory
no one wanted. The grown children

buried her quick, somewhere dry, thinking of their lives:
Sundays at the park, his kiss, those bedtime stories.

Building the House

The sound of saws, electric, chain or hand held
cut across the smell of wood. Two-by-fours arrived
for the frame, plywood over concrete,
wide pine for the floors.

My body built itself at the same
stop-start speed.
The day the windows came I bought my first bra.
Before the decks were done Patrick next door
had asked me to the dance.
His hand was sweaty, but steady
and I held it all evening long.

Father cut the wood, wielded the plum line
and drove in nails with hands shaking.
Sometimes, a few drinks in,
he'd go back after dark to take a look,
the shell transforming,
the shape suddenly solid and strong.

Her Blue Room

has not made the journey with her
to this day.
The wooden chair and chest
shift to the left.
Now to the right.
Her balance adjusts itself,
but gets it wrong.
If she walks quickly,
as if with no effort,
there is a way
into these walls again.
The room is here
where she left it,
but she is nowhere to be found.

Bridge

I got the clock, you the pots.
The only thing I wanted?
The small dish
blue as the sky over Prague,
its stumpy legs like udders.
Its markings orange as that café
the one with the tall proud hostess,
asparagus easy as butter,
where the air was still
nothing happened
and I thought only of your hands.

Don't be Mad

It could end like this: soft wind and rain on your face.
Or not. Tom's dad dead at 52 from too much of too much.
How do we know when to stop, much less how?

No way to choose the end. But if you could?
Surely music, fragrant violin or a crashing of piano keys.
People weeping of course, lots of them and mostly men
lacerating their hearts with memories of you golden.

You'd never end it alone and old, drunk
again, in a bar, some Midwest town late at night, saying:
Don't be mad Mister, I just wanted to touch your face.

An Error of Timing

One morning
maybe you slept in.
Or there was a wedding
you forgot to attend.
Some small
error of timing
has brought you here
and you don't recognise
the colour of this stone.

Turn back,
ask directions of the man
selling melons
at the side of the road.
He doesn't know,
but says the melons are ripe.
The woman with the baby
signs to keep going
until you reach the sea.

Newport Parrog

for Kate Griffin

Even dry leaves
find a way of dancing here,
caught up in waves
of Indian Summer.
A sky meant for Greece
unfolds day after day.
They made it without clouds
as clear as an infant's eye.

A look inside my suitcase tells all:
I expected rain, storms even,
shades of grey for certain.
This child who has awoken,
stretched herself into these lost hot days
finds herself naked, unprepared.

Widow

At the back of her mind lay summers
walking the beach with Henry.
At the front icicles formed,
melted slightly, reformed.
At night she clung to the patchwork quilt
until the gulls' call at sunrise.

I remember her blue still eyes
and her slender shaking hands.
On the way to school and back
I'd wave to her at the window
bringing her news or wild flowers
when I could.

Last summer I carved her name
into a bench above the bay.
From there you can watch the gulls
as they follow the tugs
each evening coming home.

In the Bedroom

The only colour in the room—
a vase the blue a baby's eyes might be.
What prepares you for such longing?

Mornings she searches the garden
for new growth. Today late summer
Michaelmas daisies tease with their lilac flowers.

Lilac is a healing colour
and she is not ready, yet.
There will be years still of this whiteness

which is not white, but an absence
of heat. Afternoons she paces
through all the rooms,

strains the hues from walls
painted in brighter times,
leaving a faint and bitter chill.

Frozen

I often think of you when I am alone on my bus
watching the frozen brown fields warming
in the morning sun while commuters sleep all around me.

I think of the long scarf you wore last winter,
how it distracted me, being so close
to your skin, so easily wrapped around you.

I think too of what I might say if I had the chance
and how it would be to take your hands
into mine and have them all around me.

Bakerloo Line

As if they know a silence
has just been broken—
no one speaks, even the usual clack
of the old train hushes itself.
Oxford Circus, Regents Park, Baker Street.
I want to say more, but stations
rush past us, and everyone is so still.
Marylebone, Edgware Road.

Warwick Avenue? We jump off, double back
to Paddington and our lives,
laughing at how easy it is
to miss a stop and to miss a chance
and how the Bakerloo line
will never be the same again.

Paddington Station

The familiar smell of diesel,
fast food and stale air.
The same stalls selling
Paddington Bears and jellybeans.
People zigzagging past
with briefcases or backpacks.
The click of high heels
and drone of announcements.
The 19.10 from Swansea is leaving
from Platform eight they say.
This scene is exactly as it always was
except we are standing here together
neither of us knowing
which way to go.

Christ Church Meadow

The two ducks that wandered by
and the American couple sprawled along the grass
may have heard a word or two of what I said to you
fifty miles away in London,
but they each had their own preoccupations and so
may not have seen my sudden smile
at hearing you say *us*.

Through all the starts and stops and grinding gear changes
of the bus ride home I smiled on.
This unexpected heat
and weeks of blue skies would be enough
to explain my smile, but halfway there I looked around
to check if anyone had noticed. The driver was new and young
and watched the road. The man behind me slept.

Gift

In my room at midnight I hold your gift,
unwrap it for the second time—

undo the bright ribbon and remove the paper
to reveal the fire-like colour of the dish.

Quietly I trace my fingers over the smooth surface,
moistening them to remove a little glue the label left.

Outside the moon is half-full and the church steeple
rises against a troubled sky.

First

Where you kissed me
wild flowers are blossoming—

cornflowers first then rain daisies.
By midday buttercups and honeysuckle.

It is evening now and still more come.
Love, I have never seen

such deep colours—
ruby, indigo, damson.

Each petal is as soft
as the look in your eyes

the first time
we tried to say goodbye.

St Martin's Island

I

As for what I found:
Agapanthus and Whistling Jacks,
clear water and birds in no hurry.
Pots of carnations beside the road—
fifty pence a bunch—church doors open
and bikes unchained.
Early on a lack of horns and sirens.
A few days in I recognised a Stonechat
from a Wren and directed a day-tripper
to the chapel of rest or its remains.

II

A dolphin skeleton
washed up on Par beach yesterday.
Yellow moss covers roofs and rocks.

Mary sells cakes with purple ribbons for the Jubilee.
We watch the floats—a lighthouse, a crown,
and the Mad Hatter's Tea Party
make their way along the main, and only, road
then turn for Higher Town quay.
My husband is having trouble containing me,
a woman says to her friend.
Joe cannot say when the boat will sail on Saturday—
It depends on so many things.
Gold balloons escape throughout the afternoon.

Here, Now

This is how far east
my east needs to be.
What else is there to say?
To speak of liquid green land
with beer so dark
it draws you in,
and the smiles not easily won,
takes so long, so many years
of learning to recount.
Gardens I called yards
the pushing at the door
opening
only when I stopped.

Visit

I'm folding socks when you appear.
In that deep voice I've missed
you comment on the weather. *Eighty-six degrees!*
I hear myself offer everything—ice water, lemons,
that pressed apple juice from Waitrose.

Just stand there in the light,
lift your skirt a little.
So nothing's changed then I'm laughing,
but I see your hand tremble as it traces my thigh.

I turn for you to unbutton me
while I watch the daisies outside in the wind.
It's a moment before I realise I'm still dressed,
the room emptier.

San Xavier Mission

Is that all, the Mexican waitress asks
meaning: *Is this all my life is?*
It's morning, Arizona, and the sun
welcomes you to San Xavier Mission
where at the parking lot edge
you can eat fried dough with honey
warm enough to warm your soul,
softened, in spite of yourself, by 100 candles
burning in the church, doors open
and a breeze blowing in.

Mountains surround you here
as everywhere you've been for days
which explains, perhaps, this crazy
need to escape, to run up into the hills
to find out what your life is.

Filling Mia

We are filling you up
spooning in a view of the sea,
a moment bouncing on a
green garden chair,
being tossed up
against a big blue Norfolk sky.

Open your mouth,
let us fill you
with a walk along the quay,
fifty sailboats tipping their sails,
crabs in a bucket,
cakes by the beach at the caravan café.

There are hungers coming.
These days will always be there
jumbled together—
crabs and skies and sails
and I will not.

Blakeney, Norfolk

Standing here beside the Estuary
watching the tides go out
I should be watching you,
but I'm thinking again of all I'll say
one day—oh, about men perhaps—
the way I first noticed their hands,
how their hands always give them away.

Or, how, despite everything, they're worth it.
Maybe, if you catch me off guard on a warm night
like tonight—the first blue sky in a week—
I might be more specific, name names.
I'll tell you one day, say at sixteen
(that was a good year) not to be afraid to choose—
indecision is only a fear of death.

Choose a place, but travel often.
Choose a man early, but not the one
you think you can't live without.
He'll leave you babbling to yourself
midnight in a town with no cinema.
One day you'll see I've told you not to live my life
and what will that tell you?

Driving Cornwall

This day is a mug of tea. Warm.
Seagulls welcome you to town.
The man who runs the B&B smiles
so easily you know this bed
will be firm and the pillows thick.
When you eat it is at a café by the beach
where even the sausages taste
as if someone cared.

A ginger cat brushes round your legs
as you climb the hill to watch
the evening settle in and lights come on.
You've never seen so many stars.
This seems like a return—
that taste of salt in the air
tells your bones this is home.
There are six more days.

Time to Go Now

Pack up the papers, books
the notes and addresses of those
you might see again.
Take what you can,
even the shells,
the white stone with its thin red line,
the sea glass and museum ticket stubs.
Take the half-written postcards,
the dress with the daring neckline.
Take the recipe for Khorta,
the film to be developed,
the wooden bracelet for your mother.

Take it with you,
there will be a time for travelling light.